The month of March, from the illuminated manuscript
Les Très Riches Heures du duc de Berry

The Story of a Special Day
Volume 85

March

25

84th day of the year
(85th in leap years)
281 days remaining
until the end of the year.

by Michael Dobson

Timespinner
Press

For more information about the series, about me, or about your special day, please email us at editor@timespinnerpress.com.

Look for other volumes in *The Story of a Special Day*, coming often.

Table of Contents

Cover: Detail from a Venice travel poster; for the founding of the city of Venice on March 25, 421, the Event of the Day.

Back Cover and Frontispiece: The month of March, from the French Gothic illuminated manuscript *Les Très Riches Heures du duc de Berry*.

March 25 Quotations

"I am who I am, I am what I am, I do what I do, and I ain't never gonna do it any different. I don't care who likes it and who don't."

— *country singer Buck Owens, died March 25, 2006*

"That's the beauty of this country — we can have different opinions and coexist and be amused by each other and hurt and offended."

— *actress Sarah Jessica Parker, born March 25, 1965*

"It's very important to have two tiaras when you're on the road, you never know when you'll be invited to something really formal."

— *musician Elton John, born March 25, 1947*

"It's astounding, time is fleeting, madness takes its toll."

— Rocky Horror Show *author Richard O'Brien who played Riff Raff in the film version, born March 25, 1942*

"If the shoe doesn't fit, must we change the foot?"

—feminist and author Gloria Steinem, born March 25, 1934

"DOWN GOES FRAZIER! DOWN GOES FRAZIER! DOWN GOES FRAZIER!"

—sportscaster Howard Cosell, born March 25, 1918

"The colour of my soul is iron-grey and sad bats wheel about the steeple of my dreams."

—composer Claude Debussy, died March 25, 1918

"You can't build a peaceful world on empty stomachs and human misery.

—Nobel-winning agronomist Norman Borlaug, born March 25, 1914

"Like most of those who study history, he learned from the mistakes of the past how to make new ones.

—historian A. J. P. Taylor, born March 25, 1906

Event of the Day
The Founding of Venice

Gondoliers on the Grand Canal, Venice. Photo: Saffron Blaze

While fishermen dwelled on the marshy lagoons since late Roman times, the city of Venice (Venezia) was founded (according to tradition) at the stroke of noon on March 25, 421 CE, with the dedication of the Church of San Giacomo di Rialto.

Venice is known internationally as the City of Canals. It consists of 117 islands formed by 177 canals connected by 409 bridges, and is the largest car-free urban area in Europe. Located in the extreme northeast of Italy, it borders the Adriatic Sea in the marshy Venetian Lagoon, in between the mouths of the Po and the Piave Rivers.

The city takes its name from the Veneti people who inhabited the region even before it was incorporated into the Roman empire. The first actual settlers of the swampy islands in the Venetian Lagoon were Roman refugees fleeing the Germanic and Hun invasions. After the collapse of the Western Roman Empire in 476 CE, the lagoon dwellers passed under the nominal control of the Eastern (Byzantine) Roman Empire, but their isolation gave the region a good deal of autonomy.

Because the Lombard Kingdom occupied the surrounding lands, Venice built ports and focused its attention on the sea and trade. Venice broke with the Byzantine Empire in 726 CE over the "iconoclastic controversy," a religious conflict within the Orthodox Church on the suitability of religious images, urged on by the Roman Catholic Pope Gregory II, and became independent. The *Doge* of Venice (equivalent to "duke" in English or "duce" in Italian) became the new ruler of the city.

Over the next several centuries, the Republic of Venice grew to be the leading power in Mediterranean commerce. It ruled Cyprus and Crete, dominated the salt trade, and in 1204 CE captured Constantinople. A republic with an elected ruler, it was religiously liberal, which led to frequent conflicts with the Catholic Church. Venice was the printing capital of the world and a center for symphonic and operatic music.

Venice's fortunes began to reverse in the 15th century. A thirty-year war with the Turks cost Venice many of its possessions. Venice's monopoly of east-west trade was broken when Portugal discovered a sea route to India. Plague killed nearly a third of Venice's citizens. Finally, in 1797 CE, Napoleon conquered Venice and brought an end to its independence.

Today, Venice is the capital of the Veneto region of Italy. Historic Venice is home to around 60,000 residents and a daily average of some 50,000 tourists. Its famous attractions include St. Mark's Basilica, the Grand Canal, and the Piazza San Marco. The traditional Venetian gondola is primarily for tourists or for special occasions such as weddings; waterbuses *(vaporetti)* are used for most daily purposes.

Venice is threatened by flood tides from the Adriatic, and began sinking when artesian wells began to draw too much water. Some recent studies suggest that Venice may have stabilized, but work continues to make sure the historic city is remains, as one critic put it, "undoubtedly the most beautiful city built by man."

March 25 Holidays and Celebrations

Anniversary of the Arengo (San Marino)

San Marino, completely surrounded by Italy, is the smallest republic in the world and the oldest state in Europe. On March 25, 1906, its directly elected parliament, the Arengo, took power. Each March 25, the military of San Marino appear in full-dress uniform and parade through the old town center to commemorate this event.

Feast of the Annunciation (Christianity)

March 25, nine full months before Christmas, celebrates the angel Gabriel's announcement to the Virgin Mary that she would conceive and become the mother of Jesus. It is sometimes moved to a different day if March 25 falls on a Sunday or falls during Holy Week. In England, March 25 is **Lady Day**, and was New Year's Day up until the adoption of the Gregorian calendar in 1752.

The Annunciation, by Leonardo da Vinci

Freedom Day (Belarus)

March 25 is an unofficial holiday in Belarus, commemorating the creation of the Belarusian People's Republic (BPR) on March 25, 1918. The government does not recognize the event because the BPR was created by the Germans who then occupied Belarus. People opposed to the current Belarusian government use the celebration for demonstrations and protests.

Hilaria Matris Deûm (Ancient Rome)

On the eighth day before the Kalends of April (March 25), ancient Rome honored Cybele, mother of the gods. The event was celebrated by a procession of the statue of the goddess, a display of wealth, and a wide variety of games, amusements, and masquerades. The amusements and masquerades of Hilaria gave rise to our English word "hilarious."

Maryland Day (Maryland)

The legal holiday of Maryland Day celebrates the landing of the first European settlers in the Province of Maryland on March 25, 1634.

Mother's Day (Slovenia)

Mother's Day is celebrated in Slovenia on March 25.

Revolution Day (Greece)

March 25 is the symbolic outbreak of the Greek War of Independence from the Ottoman Empire in 1821.

Struggle for Human Rights Day (Slovakia)

The peaceful Candle Demonstration against the communist government of Czechoslovakia on March 25, 1988, turned violent when the secret police attacked the crowd of over 5,000 Slovakians. Today, March 25 is commemorated in Slovakia as Struggle for Human Rights Day.

Tolkien Reading Day (The Tolkien Society, international)

March 25, the day of the fall of Sauron according to The Lord of the Rings, was chosen as Tolkien Reading Day, encouraging the reading of Tolkien's books and their use in education.

Våffeldagen (Sweden)

In Sweden, March 25 is Waffle Day. The name *Våffeldagen* sounds like *Vårfrudagen,* or "Our Lady's Day" (see "Feast of the Annunciation" above), leading to this parallel celebration.

Easter Season

Easter is a "moveable feast," meaning it occurs on different days each year. The earliest date for Easter is March 22, and all events of the Easter season adjust accordingly. See the Easter Events section for more details.

Christian Feast Days

In **Western Christianity**, March 25 is the feast day of Alfwold, Barontius and Desiderius, Dismas the "Good Thief," Humbert of Maroilles, and Quirinus of Tegernsee.

In **Eastern Orthodox Christianity**, March 25 is the Feast of the Annunciation of Our Most Holy Lady Theotokos and Ever-Virgin Mary; commemoration of the martyrs Pelagia, Theodosia, and Dula of Nicomedia; the Russian martyr Tikhon, Patriarch of Moscow; Saint Justin Popovich of Cheliye; and the repose of Hiero-schema monk Parthenins of Kiev. (These events are observed on April 7 by "Old Calendarists" who use the Julian calendar.)

What Happened on March 25?

The abbreviation "O.S." on some dates refers to the fact that the Russian Empire did not switch from the Julian to the Gregorian calendar at the same time as the rest of Europe, and therefore some figures and events have two dates.

People and events whose original names are not in the Western alphabet have their native names (where possible) in the appropriate script shown in parenthesis.

1199 CE – Richard the Lionheart is Fatally Wounded

While besieging the castle of Chalus-Chabrol in France, King Richard I Cœur de Lion of England went out to inspect the progress of his troops on the evening of March 25, 1199. He was amused at one of the castle's defenders: a man with a crossbow in one hand and a frying pan in the other, which he was using as a shield. The crossbowman shot at the king, but missed. While the king was distracted, another crossbowman was luckier, and his bolt struck Richard in the shoulder. The surgeon who removed the crossbow bolt botched the job, and Richard's wound grew gangrenous.

Richard's men captured the crossbowman, a young boy, and brought him before the king. The boy told Richard that he had killed his father and both his brothers, and had shot the king in revenge. Although he expected to be executed, Richard ordered the boy to be freed and given 100 shillings, his last act of mercy. Richard died on April 6, 1199, in the arms of his mother.

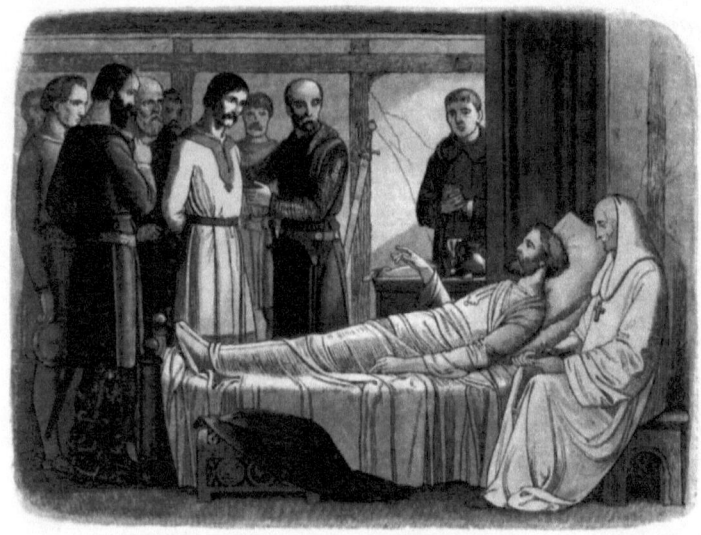

Richard I pardons the archer who shot him

1655 CE – **Discovery of Titan**

Galileo had discovered four moons orbiting the giant planet Jupiter in 1610, but the limits of telescope technology ended his explorations of the heavens. Inspired by Galileo, the Dutch astronomer

Christiaan Huygens built more powerful telescopes, and on the night of March 25, 1655, he observed Titan, the largest moon orbiting the planet Saturn. He also correctly identified the rings of Saturn for the first time.

1807 CE – End of the Slave Trade in the British Empire

On March 25, 1807, the British Parliament passed "An Act for the Abolition of the Slave Trade." Although the trade in slaves was banned, the act did not outlaw slavery itself; that would not occur until 1833. Britain did, however, pressure other countries to prohibit trade in slaves as well. The US banned Atlantic slave trading in the same month. Portugal, Sweden, France, and the Netherlands followed suit. Over fifty African rulers also agreed to stop the trade in slaves. Over the next sixty years, the Royal Navy would seize over 1,600 slave ships and free 150,000 Africans.

1807 CE – First Passenger Railway Service

The Swansea and Mumbles Railway, a horse-drawn railway line originally built to transport limestone from the quarries at Mumbles to the town of Swansea in Wales, carried the world's first fare-paying railway passengers on March 25, 1807.

It took seventy years for the horses to give way to steam engines. By the time the railway closed in 1960, it was the longest operating railway in the world and still holds the record for the most different types of propulsion: the Swansea and Mumbles had used horses, sails, steam, electric, gasoline, and diesel.

1894 CE – **First March on Washington**

The first significant protest march on Washington, DC, began in Massilon, Ohio, on March 25, 1894, reaching Washington, DC, on April 30. Known as "Coxey's Army" for its leader, Jacob Coxey, the march protested unemployment caused by the Panic of 1893, which began what was up to that time the worst economic depression in American history. One hundred men began the march, and the number grew to 6,000 jobless men by the time it reached Washington. One group of marchers took over a Northern Pacific train, fighting off federal marshals who tried to stop them. The leaders were arrested the day after their arrival in DC for walking on the grass at the United States Capitol, and the march petered out. The phrase "enough food to feed Coxey's Army" entered popular culture as a result of the march.

1911 CE – **Triangle Shirtwaist Factory Fire**

The deadliest industrial disaster in New York City history took place on March 25, 1911, when a fire broke out at the Triangle Shirtwaist Factory in Manhattan.

Because the managers had locked the doors to the stairwells and exits to prevent unauthorized breaks, the workers, mostly women, could not escape. One hundred forty-six garment workers died from the fire, smoke inhalation, or jumping to their deaths.

After the fire, legislation imposed new safety standards for factories, and the International Ladies' Garment Workers' Union grew into a powerful union fighting sweatshop conditions. A memorial to the disaster was planned at the centennial observance in 2011.

1931 CE – **Arrest of the Scottsboro Boys**

On March 25, 1931, nine black teenage boys were arrested near Scottsboro, Alabama, and charged with the rape of two white women. All but one, a 13-year old boy, were quickly convicted and sentenced to death. An appeal resulted in a new trial, in which one of the alleged victims admitted she had made up the rape story and that none of the accused had touched either of the women.

Nevertheless, the defendants were convicted of rape again, and most served lengthy prison sentences. One was shot in prison by a guard, two escaped and were recaptured, and one escaped in 1946 and remained in hiding for thirty years before being pardoned. The case is widely considered a miscarriage of justice, and led to the abolition of all-white juries in the South.

1949 CE – **The March Deportation**

For three days beginning on March 25, 1949, the Soviet Union deported nearly 90,000 Estonians, Latvians, and Lithuanians, primarily women and children, from their homeland, declaring them "enemies of the people." The deportation, code named Operation Priboi, was later declared a crime against humanity because of the high death rate, as the Soviet Union did not provide clothing or housing for those who had been deported.

1957 CE – The EEC is Established

On March 25, 1957, the Treaty of Paris established the European Economic Community (EEC), also known as the "common market," to facilitate trade and economic integration among its members. The six founding members of the EEC were Belgium, France, Italy, Luxembourg, the Netherlands, and West Germany.

Selma to Montgomery March: Children of civil rights leader Dr. Ralph Abernathy are followed by Dr. and Mrs. Martin Luther King

1965 CE – The Selma March Reaches Montgomery

Civil rights marchers protesting denial of voting rights and other aspects of segregation arrived at

the Alabama State Capitol on March 25, 1965. It was
the third attempt to complete the march. The first,
on March 7, was attacked by police in what became
known as "Bloody Sunday." The second attempt, a
week later, was forced to stop by court order. The
third march began on March 16. The march was
guarded by nearly 4,000 soldiers as well as by
numerous FBI agents and federal marshals, and
resulted in a major shift in public opinion in favor
of the civil rights movement.

John Lennon and Yoko Ono's Bed-In for Peace, March 25, 1969

1969 CE – **John and Yoko's Bed-In**

Beginning on March 25, 1969, Beatle John Lennon
and his new spouse Yoko Ono held the "Bed-Ins for
Peace," one in Amsterdam and one in Montreal.

Knowing the occasion of their wedding would result in massive publicity, the couple decided to use their honeymoon as a public opportunity to promote world peace, inviting reporters into their hotel room every day between 9am and 9pm. The event has entered popular culture and has been repeated by other artists.

1992 CE – The "Last Citizen of the USSR" Returns From Space

Cosmonaut Sergei Krikalev (Сергей Крикалёв) spent a record-setting total of 803 days in outer space in six missions. His longest mission began on May 19, 1991, when he made his second trip to the Mir space station. When he left Earth, he was a citizen of the USSR, but the Soviet Union dissolved on December 26, 1991, while he was still in space. When he returned to Earth on March 25, 1992, that nation no longer existed, and as a result Krikalev became known as the "last citizen of the USSR."

Sergei Krikalev

Who Was Born on March 25?

Art

Gutzon Borglum (March 25, 1867 — March 6, 1941)

Danish-American sculptor Gutzon Borglum is best known for his monumental work at Mount Rushmore and Stone Mountain.

Mount Rushmore sculptures by Gutzon Borglum

Business

Tom Monaghan (March 25, 1937 —)
Monaghan founded Domino's Pizza, and owned the
Detroit Tigers in the 1980s and early 1990s.

Eileen Ford (March 25, 1922 —)
Eileen Ford co-founded Ford Models, one of the
most famous modeling agencies in the world,
representing such supermodels as Christie
Brinkley, Rene Russo, and Lauren Hutton.

Film and Television

Lee Pace (March 25, 1979 —)
Pace was nominated for a Golden Globe and an
Emmy as star of the TV series *Pushing Daisies.*

Kari Matchett (March 25, 1970 —)
Matchett appeared in leading roles in *24* and *Covert
Affairs.*

Sarah Jessica Parker (March 25, 1965 —)
Parker is best known for playing Carrie Bradshaw in
the TV and film series *Sex and the City.*

Lisa Gay Hamilton (March 25, 1964 –)

Hamilton played Rebecca Washington on *The Practice* and young Sethe in the 1998 film *Beloved*.

Marcia Cross (March 25, 1962 –)

Cross played Kimberly Shaw on *Melrose Place* and Bree on *Desperate Housewives*.

Brenda Strong (March 25, 1960 –)

Strong played Mary Alice Young on the TV series *Desperate Housewives* and also appeared in the series *Sport Night* and the remake of *Dallas*.

Haywood Nelson (March 25, 1960 –)

Nelson played Dwayne on the 1970s TV series *What's Happening!!*

James McDaniel (March 25, 1958 –)

McDaniel played Lt. Fancy on *NYPD Blue* and an advisor to the lead character in 1992's *Malcolm X*.

Matthew Garber (March 25, 1956 – June 13, 1977)

Garber played the son in 1964's *Mary Poppins* and also appeared in other Disney films. He died at age 21 of pancreatitis.

Bonnie Bedelia (March 25, 1948 —)

Bedelia appeared in *Die Hard, Die Hard 2, Presumed Innocent*, and *Heart Like a Wheel*. She is the aunt of actor Macaulay Culkin.

Paul Michael Glaser (March 25, 1943 —)

Glaser played Starsky on the 1970s TV series *Starsky and Hutch*.

Paul Michael Glaser (left) and David Soul from *Starsky and Hutch*

Richard O'Brien (March 25, 1942 —)

O'Brien wrote the cult hit *The Rocky Horror Show* and appeared in the film version as the character Riff Raff.

Machiko Kyō (京 マチ子) (March 25, 1924 —)

Japanese actress Kyō is known to American audiences for her roles in *Rashomon* and *Teahouse of the August Moon*.

Roberts Blossom (March 25, 1924 — July 8, 2011)

Blossom is best known for playing the old man in *Home Alone* and for his role as Ezra Cobb in *Deranged*.

Simone Signoret (March 25, 1921 — September 30, 1985)

Simone Signoret was the first French actress to win an Academy Award. Her notable films include *Room at the Top* and *Ship of Fools*.

Patrick Troughton (March 25, 1920 — March 28, 1987)

British actor Troughton is best known for playing the Second Doctor in the long-running *Doctor Who* television series. He was also the first actor to play Robin Hood on television.

Jean Rogers (March 25, 1916 — February 24, 1991)

Jean Rogers is best remembered for playing Dale Arden in two *Flash Gordon* serials of the 1930s.

David Lean (March 25, 1908 — April 16, 1991)

Director and producer Sir David Lean is best known for such films as *The Bridge on the River Kwai, Lawrence of Arabia*, and *Doctor Zhivago*.

Ed Begley (March 25, 1901 — April 28, 1970)

Begley won an Oscar for his role in 1962's *Sweet Bird of Youth*, and appeared in such films as *12 Angry Men* and *The Unsinkable Molly Brown*. His son Ed Begley, Jr., also became an actor.

John Laurie (March 25, 1897 — June 23, 1980)

Scottish actor Laurie is best known for the role of Private Frazer in the TV sitcom *Dad's Army*, but appeared in films directed by Alfred Hitchcock and Laurence Olivier, as well as in Shakespearian theater.

Andy Clyde (March 25, 1892 — May 18, 1967)

Scottish film and television actor Andy Clyde began his career in Mack Sennett silent films, and appeared as the farmer Cully Wilson in the TV series *Lassie* and as the neighbor in the TV sitcom *The Real McCoys*.

Letters

Kate DiCamillo (March 25, 1964 —)

Newbery Medal-winning children's author Kate DiCamillo's novels *Because of Winn-Dixie* and *The Tale of Despereaux* were both adapted into movies.

Gloria Steinem (March 25, 1934 —)

Publisher, journalist, and feminist Gloria Steinem (left) co-founded *Ms.* magazine and was a leading spokeperson for the women's liberation movement of the late 1960s and 1970s. She was a founder of the National Women's Political Caucus and the Women's Media Center.

Gene Shalit (March 25, 1926 —)

Film and book critic Gene Shalit appeared on the *Today* show from 1973 to 2010.

Flannery O'Connor (March 25, 1925 — August 3, 1964)

O'Connor is known for her Southern gothic fiction, especially for such works as *Wise Blood* and "A Good Man is Hard to Find."

A. J. P. Taylor (March 25, 1906 — September 7, 1990)

Well-respected British historian Taylor became widely known through his television lectures on military and diplomatic topics.

Mary Webb (March 25, 1881 — October 8, 1927)

Mary Webb's romantic novels set in the Shropshire countryside were popular in the early years of the 20th century. Her 1917 novel *Gone to Earth* was made into a 1950 film. The 1932 comic novel by Stella Gibbons, *Cold Comfort Farm* (made into the 1995 movie of the same name) is a parody of her work.

Military and Space

James Lovell (March 25, 1928 —)

NASA astronaut and Navy captain Lovell was the first person to fly in space four times. His missions were Gemini 7, Gemini 12, Apollo 8, and Apollo 13, on which he was the mission commander.

James Lovell crew photograph from the Apollo 13 mission

Albrecht Mertz von Quirnheim (March 25, 1905 — July 21, 1944)

Von Quirheim was a member of the 20 July plot that attempted unsuccessfully to kill Adolf Hitler.

Myles Keogh (March 25, 1840 — June 25, 1876)

Irish soldier of fortune Myles Keogh fought in the 1860 Papal War in Italy and on the Union side in the American Civil War before perishing at Little Bighorn as a company commander in George Armstrong Custer's 7th Cavalry.

Myles Keogh

Music

Katherine McPhee (March 25, 1984 —)

American Idol runner-up McPhee had a gold record with her single "Over It" and had a starring role in the TV series *Smash.*

Elton John (March 25, 1947 —)

English rocker Elton John's many hits include "Candle in the Wind," "Crocodile Rock," and "Goodbye Yellow Brick Road." He was inducted into the Rock and Roll Hall of Fame in 1994 and knighted in 1988.

Aretha Franklin (March 25, 1941 —)

Known as the Queen of Soul, Franklin's hits include "R-E-S-P-E-C-T," "Chain of Fools," and "(You Make Me Feel Like) A Natural Woman."

Anita Bryant (March 25, 1940 —)

Anita Bryant had several Top 40 hits in the late 1950s and 1960s, and was later known as a spokesperson for the Florida Citrus Commission and as an outspoken critic of homosexuality.

Hoyt Axton (March 25, 1938 — October 26, 1999)

Axton was a singer-songwriter and actor, whose notable songs include "Joy to the World" and "Greenback Dollar."

Bonnie Guitar (March 25, 1923 —)

Country-pop singer Bonnie Guitar had a 1957 crossover hit with "Dark Moon."

Frankie Carle (March 25, 1903 — March 7, 2001)

Bandleader and pianist Carle, nicknamed "the wizard of the keyboard," had a 1938 number one hit with "Sunrise Serenade."

Béla Bartók (March 25, 1881 — September 26, 1945)

Hungarian composer Bartók is considered one of the most important classical composers of the 20th century. A student of folk music, he is also one of the founders of the discipline of ethnomusicology.

Arturo Toscanini (March 25, 1867 — January 16, 1957)

Conductor Arturo Toscanini was musical director of La Scala in Milan and the Metropolitan Opera in New York, and led the New York Philharmonic and the NBC Symphony Orchestra, which made him widely known to the general public.

Newsmakers

Melita Norwood (March 25, 1912 — June 2, 2005)

British civil servant Norwood (code name "Hola") provided state secrets to the KGB for forty years, and was considered the most important female ever recruited by Soviet intelligence. Her role was revealed publicly in 1999. She was never prosecuted.

Jack Ruby (March 25, 1911 — January 3, 1967)

Dallas nightclub owner Jack Ruby famously shot and killed Lee Harvey Oswald, assassin of President John F. Kennedy (next page). He died of lung cancer while awaiting a retrial of his murder conviction.

Horatio Nelson Jackson (March 25, 1872 — January 14, 1955)

With his driving partner Sewall Crocker, Jackson was the first to drive an automobile across the United States. The trip from California to New York took 63 days in a Winton automobile called the *Vermont*.

Jack Ruby (foreground, with hat and gun), shooting Lee Harvey Oswald

Science

Norman Borlaug (March 25, 1914 — September 12, 2009)

Nobel-prize winning agronomist Norman Borlaug has been called "the father of the Green Revolution" and "the man who saved a billion lives" for his work in developing high-yield, disease resistant wheat varieties that have saved over a billion people worldwide from starvation.

Christopher Clavius (March 25, 1538 — February 6, 1612)

Jesuit mathematician and astronomer Christopher Clavius designed the modern Gregorian calendar, which remains in use today. The third-largest visible crater on the Moon is named Clavius in his honor.

Christopher Clavius, by Francesco Villamena

Sports

Danica Patrick (March 25, 1982 —)

Patrick is the most successful woman in the history of American open-wheel racing, holding the highest finish by a woman at the Indianapolis 500.

Sheryl Swoopes (March 25, 1971 —)

Olympic gold medalist basketball player Swoopes was the first player signed in the WNBA, and has been called "the female Michael Jordan."

Tom Glavine (March 25, 1966 —)

Atlanta Braves pitcher Glavine was a two-time Cy Young Award winner and one of only 6 left-handed pitchers to earn 300 career wins.

Avery Johnson (March 25, 1965 —)

Known as the "Little General," Johnson was both a professional basketball player and coach of two NBA teams.

Alex Solis (March 25, 1964 —)

Jockey Alex Solis won the 1986 Preakness among many other major racing wins, and is a member of the Calder Race Course Hall of Fame.

Mark Brooks (March 25, 1961 —)

Golfer Mark Brooks won the 1996 PGA Championship.

Ray Tanner (March 25, 1958 —)

Tanner became athletic director of the University of South Carolina after 16 seasons as head baseball coach. He was named National Coach of the Year in 2000, 2010, and 2011.

Lee Mazzilli (March 25, 1955 —)

Former center fielder and first baseman Lee Mazzilli testified before a grand jury in the Pittsburgh drug trials, and subsequently managed the Baltimore Orioles.

Howard Cosell (March 25, 1918 — April 23, 1995)

Legendary sportscaster Howard Cosell (next page) rose to fame covering the boxing career of Muhammad Ali and hosted *Monday Night Football* for many years.

Irving Baxter (March 25, 1876 — June 13, 1957)

Baxter won two gold and three silver medals in the high jump, pole vault, and standing jump competitions in the 1900 Paris Olympic Games.

Howard Cosell

Who Died on March 25?

Art

Wilhelm Marstrand (December 24, 1810 – March 25, 1873)

Marstrand is one of the most famous artists of the Golden Age of Danish Painting, and is ranked as perhaps the greatest Danish painter of all time.

Film and Television

Angelines Fernández (July 9, 1922 – March 25, 1994)

Star of Mexican film and television, Fernández is best known for her role as Doña Cleotilde on the sitcom *El Chavo*.

Nancy Walker (May 10, 1922 – March 25, 1992)

Actress and director Nancy Walker is remembered for her role as the mother of the lead character in the TV series *Rhoda* and as the housekeeper on *McMillan & Wife*.

Portrait of Eggert Christopher Tryde by Wilhelm Marstrand

Robert Newton (June 1, 1905 — March 25, 1956)

Newton played Long John Silver in the Disney film version of Treasure Island. His exaggerated West Country accent became the standard "pirate voice," and he is the patron saint of the International Talk Like a Pirate Day, celebrated each September 19.

Government

Faisal bin Abdulaziz Al Saud (فيصل بن عبدالعزيز آل سعو) (April 1906 — March 25, 1975)

King Faisal of Saudi Arabia ruled from 1964 to 1975, stabilizing the kingdom's finances and leading efforts for modernization and reform. He was assassinated by his nephew in 1975.

Letters

James Wright (December 13, 1927 — March 25, 1980)

American poet Wright won the Pulitzer Prize for his 1972 *Collected Poems*. The annual James Wright Poetry Festival in Martins Ferry Ohio was held every year from 1981 to 2007.

Music

Buck Owens (August 12, 1929 — March 25, 2006)

Country star Buck Owens pioneered the Bakersfield sound and co-hosted the long-running TV series *Hee Haw*. He is in the Country Music Hall of Fame and the Nashville Songwriters Hall of Fame.

(left to right) Buck Owens, Lisa Todd, and Roy Clark from *Hee Haw*

Robert Joffrey (December 24, 1930 — March 25, 1988)

Robert Joffrey co-founded the Joffrey Ballet. He is a member of the National Museum of Dance Hall of Fame.

Claude Debussy (August 22, 1862 — March 25, 1918)

French Impressionist composer Claude Debussy's famous works include *Prélude à l'après-midi d'un faune (Prelude to the Afternoon of a Faun)*.

Portrait of Claude Debussy by Marcel Baschet

Science and Medicine

James Braid (June 19, 1795 — March 25, 1860)

Scottish physician Braid is known as the first genuine hypnotherapist and the "father of modern hypnotism."

Sports

Cal Ripken, Sr. (December 17, 1935 — March 25, 1999)

Player, scout, coach and manager Cal Ripken, Sr., spent 36 years in the Baltimore Orioles organization, and became the first and only father to manage two sons (Cal Ripken, Jr., and Billy Ripken) in the major leagues.

Bob Waterfield (July 26, 1920 — March 25, 1983)

Pro Football Hall of Fame quarterback Bob Waterfield played for the Cleveland/Los Angeles Rams from 1945 to 1952, and subsequently coached for the Rams. He was married to actress Jane Russell, a high school classmate, from 1943 to 1968.

Lou Moore (September 12, 1904 — March 25, 1956)

Racecar driver Lou Moore drove in the Indianapolis 500 from 1928 to 1936, starting on the pole position in 1932.

Eddie Collins (May 2, 1887 — March 25, 1951)

Baseball Hall of Famer Eddie "Cocky" Collins played for the Philadelphia Athletics and the Chicago White Sox from 1906 to 1930, one of only 29 players in baseball history to have appeared in MLB games in four different decades. He is considered the greatest second baseman of all time using the win shares statistical rating system.

1910 E104 baseball card of Eddie Collins

March: The Third Month

"Up from the sea, the wild north wind is blowing
Under the sky's gray arch;
Smiling I watch the shaken elm boughs, knowing
It is the wind of March."

— *"March," John Greenleaf Whittier*

In ancient Rome, March was the first month of the year. As the first month of spring, in the Mediterranean climate it marked the beginning of the military campaign season. That's why March (Martius) is named in honor of Mars, the Roman god of war.

Although the first month of the year was moved back to January sometime during the transition of Rome from a kingdom to a republic (historians differ), March was the first month of the year in Russia until the end of the 15th Century, and is the first month of the year in many other cultures and religions.

In the northern hemisphere, March 1 marks the beginning of meteorological spring. In the southern hemisphere, March is the equivalent of September, making southern hemisphere March the beginning of autumn.

March is one of the seven months that have 31 days in it. March starts on the same day of the week as November every year, and except for leap years starts on the same day as February. March starts on the same day of the week as the previous June except for leap years, and in leap years starts on the same day as the previous September and December.

March in Other Cultures

In Finland, March is called *maaliskuu* (earthy month). In Ukraine, it's *березень* (birch tree). Other names for March include *Lentmonat* (Saxon), *Hyld-monath* (Angles), and *sušec* (Slovene).

March Symbols

Birthstones: Aquamarine and bloodstone, both representing courage.

Aquamarine

Birth Flowers: Daffodils

Daffodil

March Events

Honorary months

Presidents, Congresses, and nations around the world issue proclamations recognizing particular months to honor certain causes. These events generally fall in March. (All US unless otherwise noted.)

- National Nutrition Month
- American Red Cross Month
- Women's History Month (celebrated in Canada during October)

- Irish-American Heritage Month
- Colorectal Cancer Awareness Month
- Fire Prevention Month (The Philippines)

"March Madness" (United States)

The NCAA Men's Division I Basketball Championship, popularly known as "March Madness" or the "Big Dance," is a single-elimination tournament to establish the champion college basketball team.

Movable Events

Seward's Day (Alaska)

Seward's Day, on the last Monday in March, commemorates the signing of the Alaska Purchase Treaty on March 30, 1867. The earliest it can occur is March 25 and the latest is March 31.

Birkat Hachama (ברכת החמה) (Judaism)

According to the Talmud, the Sun was created at the vernal equinox position at the beginning of the Jewish month of Nisan, established by tradition as March 25 on the Julian calendar.

The Birkat Hachama, "Blessing of the Sun" is recited when the vernal equinox occurs at sundown on a Tuesday, which happens every 28 years.

When the Julian calendar gave way to the Gregorian calendar in 1582, the date shifted forward, and continues to shift slowly forward by approximately a day per century.

Birkat Hachma took place on April 8, 2009 (14 Nisan 5769), and will occur next on April 8, 2037 (23 Nisan 5797).

Earth Hour (International)

On Earth Hour, held on the last Saturday of March each year, households and business are urged to turn off all non-essential lights for one hour between 8:30pm to 9:30pm on each person's local time. The goal is to raise awareness of the need to take action on climate change.

Easter Events

La crucifixión by El Greco

Easter Season

The Christian holiday of Easter in Western Christianity is held on the first Sunday after the Paschal Full Moon following the March equinox, which is officially set at March 21 by church reckoning. Easter itself can therefore occur as early as March 22 and as late as April 25, but occurs most often in April. In Eastern Christianity, which uses the Julian calendar, Easter occurs between April 4 and May 8. This also sets the date for the various events that lead up to Easter, most importantly the events of Holy Week.

Passion Sunday

The fifth Sunday of the Christian season of Lent is known as Passion Sunday in various Protestant denominations and by some traditionalist Catholics. Sometimes, the sixth Sunday of Lent is referred to as Passion Sunday, but it is more commonly known as Palm Sunday.

Passion Sunday starts the two-week Passiontide, which ends on Holy Saturday, the day before Easter, commemorating the day that Jesus's body was laid in the tomb. The fifth Sunday of Lent can occur as early as March 8 (though the next time it will be that early is in 2285 CE), and as late as April 11.

Palm Sunday

The moveable feast of Palm Sunday commemorates the triumphant entry of Jesus into Jerusalem, an event mentioned in all four gospels. In many Christian churches, palm leaves are distributed to the worshippers. The earliest date for Palm Sunday is March 15, and the latest is April 18.

Maundy Thursday

The Thursday before Easter is Maundy Thursday, when the Last Supper took place. Because of its relation to Easter, the earliest day it can occur is March 19, and the latest it can occur is April 22.

Good Friday

Good Friday, observed during Holy Week on the Friday preceding Easter Sunday, commemorates the crucifixion of Jesus and his death at Calvary. Because of its relation to Easter, the earliest day it can occur is March 20, and the latest it can occur is April 23.

Holy Saturday

Sometimes called Easter Eve or Black Saturday,
Holy Saturday commemorates the day in which
Jesus's body lay in the tomb. Some mistakenly refer
to this day as "Easter Saturday," but that properly
describes the Saturday following Easter, the last day
of Easter Week. The earliest it can occur is March
21, and the latest it can occur is April 24.

Easter Eggs

Easter

Easter celebrates the resurrection of Jesus
Christ on the third day after his crucifixion.

In the liturgical calendar, Easter follows the season of Lent, and begins the period known as Eastertide, which ends on Pentecost Sunday. Easter is observed religiously in a morning service.

In the U.S., it's also common to decorate Easter eggs and make Easter baskets of eggs and candy, often with the Easter bunny as a symbol. The White House traditionally hosts an egg hunt, and many communities have Easter parades.

Easter customs around the world include bonfires (Cyprus, western Sweden), men spanking women with a ceremonial whip (Czech Republic and Slovakia), egg fighting (Bulgaria), cross-country skiing and reading murder mysteries (Norway), and children dressed as witches collecting candy door-to-door (other Nordic countries).

Easter Monday

In some Roman Catholic and Eastern Orthodox cultures, the Monday after Easter is celebrated as a holiday.

It is also known in some countries as **Egg Nyte**, featuring egg rolling competitions and dousing other people with water that had been blessed with holy water the previous day at mass.

Easter Monday is also celebrated as **Family Day** in South Africa. In Guyana, people fly kites that were made on Holy Saturday. In Portugal, it is known as the **Anjo** (**Ivy**) **Festival**, in which people picnic in the countryside.

Śmigus-Dyngus (Poland, Hungary, Czech Republic, Slovakia)

The Monday after Easter in Poland and in the Polish diaspora is known as *Śmigus-Dyngus,* or simply Dyngus Day in the US. Boys throw water over girls they like and spank them with pussy willows. Girls avoid getting wet by giving boys "ransoms" of painted eggs.

Easter Week (Western Christianity), Bright Week (Eastern Christianity)

The period from Easter Sunday to the following Saturday is known as **Easter Week**. In both Western and Eastern Christianity (where it's known as **Bright Week**), the resurrection continues to be celebrated in church services. **Easter Tuesday** is a public holiday in the Australian state of Tasmania.

March Zodiac Signs

From the perspective of someone on Earth, the Sun appears to move through the sky throughout the year, along a path astronomers call the ecliptic plane. The ecliptic plane is divided into twelve constellations, known as the zodiac, based on traditionally observed patterns of stars. On your birthday, you can't see your constellation, because it's part of the daytime sky.

The zodiac was first developed by Babylonian astronomers about 2,500 years ago. Because they were unaware that the Earth wobbles like a spinning top (a motion known as *precession*), they didn't make allowance for the fact that the Sun's path through the zodiac changes over time.

That means there are now two sets of dates for your birth sign. The *tropical* dates are the original Babylonian dates; the *siderial* dates tell you where the Sun actually appears as it moves along its annual path.

In siderial reckoning, March 25 is in Pisces, but in tropical astrology, March 25 is in Aries.

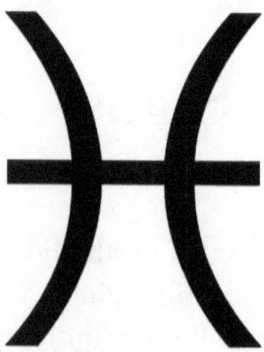

Pisces

Tropical February 20 to March 20

Siderial March 15 to April 14

In the Roman legend of Venus and her son Cupid, they escaped the clutches of Typhon, known as the "father of all monsters," by transforming into fish and tying themselves together with rope. That's why the name Pisces is plural for fish. The constellation appears as a somewhat ragged "V" shape, representing the rope, with the "fish" located at the two rope ends.

In astrology, Pisces is a water sign, compatible with the other water signs Cancer and Scorpio, as well as with the earth signs Taurus, Virgo, and Capricorn. Pisceans are supposed to be imaginative, compassionate, unworldly, secretive, and escapist.

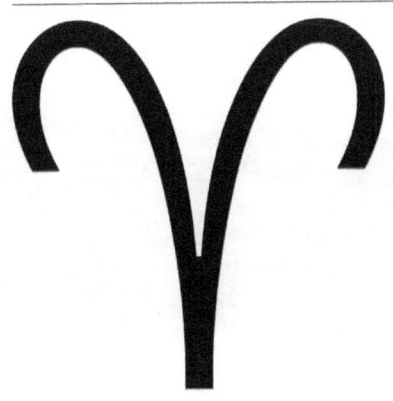

Aries

Tropical March 21 to April 19

Siderial April 15 to May 15

In Greek mythology, Aries is a ram with golden wings and golden wool who rescued the twins Phrixus and Helle from certain death. Although Helle died in the rescue attempt, the grateful Phrixus sacrificed the ram to Zeus. The golden fleece from the sacrificed ram played a prominent part in the later myth of Jason and the Argonauts.

In astrology, Aries, a fire sign, is compatible with the other fire signs of Gemini, Leo, and Sagittarius, and to a lesser extent with air signs Scorpio and Libra. Arians are supposed to be adventurous, enthusiastic, quick-tempered, and impulsive.

Illustration by Edward Penfield

What Day of the Week is March 25?

On what day of the week does March 25 fall?

Surprisingly, this isn't an easy question. Because the calendar year is 365 days long (366 in leap years), it doesn't divide evenly by the seven days of the week.

Also, the Earth goes around the Sun in about 365-1/4 days, so a calendar tends to drift over time. That's why the same date falls on different weekdays in different years.

This is made even more complicated by a change in calendars that took place in 1582. Our modern calendar has its roots in ancient Rome, in a calendar reform conducted by Julius Caesar. Caesar commissioned mathematicians to attack the problem, and came up with the idea of *leap years,* and thus standardized the calendar for centuries to come. This was called the *Julian calendar.*

Over time, however, the small errors in Caesar's calculation compounded. That's why Pope Gregory XIII commissioned the *Gregorian calendar,* used in most of the world today. Some countries converted in 1582, when the calendar was first developed; some converted later; other still haven't changed.

Gregorian and Julian aren't the only types of calendars. The Hebrew year, the Islamic year, and many other calendars are used in different parts of the world and among different people.

You can convert Gregorian dates to other calendars, including the Hebrew calendar, the Islamic calendar, and even the Mayan calendar by visiting the Fourmilab Calendar Converter at http://www.fourmilab.ch/documents/calendar/.

A 50-year brass perpetual calendar.

Copyright, Credit, and Contact

Follow Us

Our blog Dobson's Improbable History features short articles on events and people associated with each day, and updates several times each week. Get the latest on Twitter @SidewiseThinker.

Contact Us

Find an error or a format problem? Want information about the series, about us, or about when the volume for your special day might be available? Please email us at editor@timespinnerpress.com.

Sources and Art Credits

We owe a great debt to Wikipedia, which is our first stop for research. We attempt to make independent confirmation of all important dates and facts through a variety of other sources.

All art and photographs are either in the public domain or used under a Creative

Commons license, and most frequently come from Wikimedia Commons. Attribution is provided where requested by the copyright owner or when of historical significance, listed below.

- The cover illustration is taken from a 1920s travel poster in the collection of the Library of Congress Prints and Photographs Division. It was originally published by Ente Natzionale per le Industrie Turistiche, and is in the public domain because its copyright has expired.

- The illustration of the month of March used on the back cover and in the interior is from the French Gothic illuminated manuscript *Les Très Riches Heures du duc de Berry* by the Limbourg Brothers, Jean Colombe, and an intermediate painter whose name is lost to history. It is in the public domain because its copyright has expired.

- The photograph "Rialto Gondoliers" was taken by Saffron Blaze in 2011, and is used here under the Creative Commons Attribution-Share Alike 3.0 Unported license. It is both a Featured Image and a Quality Image on Wikimedia Commons.

- Leonardo da Vinci's *Annunciazione* is in the public domain because its copyright has expired. This image is courtesy of the Google Art Project, and the original painting is in the Uffizi Gallery in Florence, Italy.

- The illustration of Richard I pardoning the archer who shot him is from *A Chronicle of England: BC 55 − AD 1485* by J.W.E. Doyle, first published in 1864. It is in the public domain because its copyright has expired.

- The photograph of the Triangle Shirtwaist Fire is from the front page of the March 26, 1911 issue of the New York *World*. It is in the public domain because its copyright has expired.

- The photograph of the Selma to Montgomery March is from the family collection of civil rights leader Dr. Ralph

David Abernathy, and the three children in the foreground are Donzaleigh, Ralph III, and Juandalynn Abernathy. It was released into the public domain by the copyright holder.

- The photograph of John Lennon and Yoko Ono from the first day of their Amsterdam Bed-In for Peace is from the collection of the Nationaal Archief, The Netherlands, and is used here under the Creative Commons Attribution-Share Alike 3.0 Netherlands license.

- The training photograph of cosmonaut Sergei Krikalev is in the public domain as a work of NASA.

- The National Park Service photograph of Mount Rushmore is in the public domain as a work of the US government.

- The publicity photograph from the TV series *Starsky and Hutch* is in the public domain because it was published in the US between 1923 and 1977 without a copyright notice.

- The photograph of Gloria Steinem was taken by a *U.S. News & World Report* staff photographer, and is part of a collection donated by the magazine to the Library of Congress. As part of the deed of gift, all rights in these photographs were dedicated to the public.

- The official photograph of James Lovell from the Apollo 13 mission is in the public domain as a work of NASA.

- The 1872 photograph of Miles Keogh is in the public domain because its copyright has expired.

- The photograph of Jack Ruby shooting Lee Harvey Oswald was taken by *Dallas Morning News* photographer Jack Beers, Jr. It is in the public domain because its copyright was not renewed.

- The 1606 engraving of Christopher Clavius by Francesco Villamena is in the public domain because its copyright has expired.

- The publicity photograph of Howard Cosell from *Monday*

Night Football is in the public domain because it was published in the US between 1923 and 1977 without a copyright notice.

- Wilhelm Marstrand's 1858 portrait of Eggert Christopher Tryde is in the public domain because the original painting's copyright has expired and the photographer has released his image into the public domain.

- The publicity photograph of Buck Owens, Lisa Todd, and Roy Clark from *Hee Haw* is in the public domain because it was published in the US between 1923 and 1977 without a copyright notice.

- The 1884 portrait of Claude Debussy by Marcel Baschet is in the public domain because its copyright has expired. The original can be seen in the Bibliothèque nationale de France.

- The 1910 E104 baseball card of Eddie Collins is in the public domain because its copyright has expired.

- The photograph of aquamarine has been released into the public domain.

- The photograph of a daffodil is by Javier Martin and is used under the Creative Commons Attribution-Share Alike 3.0 Unported license.

- The 1917 Women's Suffrage demonstration comes from the Library of Congress, Prints and Photographs Division, LC-USZ62-31799 DLC, and is in the public domain because its copyright has expired.

- The painting *La crucifixión* by El Greco is located in the Museo del Prado. It is in the public domain because its copyright has expired.

- The photograph of Czechoslovakian Easter eggs was taken by Jan Kameníček, who has released the image into the public domain.

- The 50-year perpetual calendar photograph is in the public domain.